CM0074192З

MILTON KEYNES
THEN & NOW

IN COLOUR

MARION HILL

The
History
Press

First published in 2012

The History Press
The Mill, Brimscombe Port
Stroud, Gloucestershire, GL5 2QG
www.thehistorypress.co.uk

© Marion Hill, 2012

The right of Marion Hill to be identified as the Author
of this work has been asserted in accordance with the
Copyrights, Designs and Patents Act 1988.

All rights reserved. No part of this book may be reprinted
or reproduced or utilised in any form or by any electronic,
mechanical or other means, now known or hereafter invented,
including photocopying and recording, or in any information
storage or retrieval system, without the permission in writing
from the Publishers.
British Library Cataloguing in Publication Data.
A catalogue record for this book is available from the British Library.

ISBN 978 0 7524 7007 8

Typesetting and origination by The History Press
Printed in India.

CONTENTS

ACKNOWLEDGEMENTS

LIVING ARCHIVE (www.livingarchive.org.uk) provided most of the older images. This unique city repository of old photographs and collected memories is a treasure. See its linked heritage websites including the 'Clutch Club' websites created by parents and children in sixty local schools, run by Living Archive and the Open University (http://clutch.open.ac.uk/schools); and see also the websites created by its customised IT training courses: My Heritage, My Recollections, My Home Front, My Memories and My Webpage.

THE PARKS TRUST (www.theparkstrust.com) was the source of a number of the newer images – not only does it safeguard the city's open spaces, it is a reservoir of wonderful photographs.

Thanks also to the following organisations for providing photographs or information: Community Action MK (www.communityactionmk.org); Discover Milton Keynes (www.discovermiltonkeynes. co.uk); Loughton Manor First School (www.loughtonmanorfirstschool.co.uk); Milton Keynes Council (www.milton-keynes.gov.uk); Milton Keynes Dons (www.mkdons.com); Milton Keynes Heritage Association (www.mkheritage.co.uk); Milton Keynes Museum (www.mkmuseum.org.uk); Milton Keynes Theatre (www.mkweb.co.uk/mktheatre); The Open University (www.open-unversity.co.uk); The Territorial Army, Milton Keynes (www.tanearyou.org.uk).

A small number of older photographs have been reprinted from the books *Memories of Milton Keynes* (The History Press, 2008) and *Bradwell Past and Present* (Sutton, 1997), for which thanks go to Milton Keynes Development Corporation, whose function was ultimately taken over by the Homes and Community Agency with Milton Keynes Partnership (MKDC/CNT/EP archive).

Finally, particular thanks for their individual help and support go to Lizzie Bancroft, Shane Downer, Pam Duggan, David Foster, Mel Jeavons, Jane Matthews, Corrina Milner, Deborah Saunders, Mike Scott-Hyde, Clare Ward, Claire Walton, Simon Wilkinson, and especially Bob Hill for taking most of the modern photographs.

ABOUT THE AUTHOR

Marion Hill is passionate about Milton Keynes and its heritage. A Londoner by birth, she came to the city in 1972, and has lived and worked in the area ever since. Her eighteen books include *Bletchley Park People*, *Memories of Milton Keynes* and, most recently, *Bradwell Then & Now* (all The History Press). Much of Marion's inspiration for these local history books comes from the massive archive now largely held online at Living Archive (www.livingarchive.org.uk).

INTRODUCTION

'It can be said that we are all foreigners in Milton Keynes.'
(Samuel Wong in an interview for The People's History at Living Archive)

People living in the designated area of Milton Keynes forty-five years ago came under the auspices of three towns, thirteen villages and Buckinghamshire County Council. Milton Keynes Development Corporation (MKDC) was the Government-sponsored organisation whose remit was to build a new city. As the nation's last 'new town' and first New City to be designated under the 1946 New Towns Act, Milton Keynes formally came into being on 23 January 1967.

Around 40,000 people were living in the area then, in mixed occupations, from farming and small trades to some larger profitable businesses, although the two major industries of the city area – the railway works and the brickyards – seemed to be in decline. The main north-south national transport links of the M1 and the West Coast railway line allowed their traffic to hurtle through without a pause.

MKDC had been entrusted with developing a city that was self-sufficient and sufficiently well-appointed to become a regional centre. The challenge was to convert over 100sq km (40 square miles) of gently undulating land prone to flooding into modern urban spaces. Vast engineering feats, of balancing lakes, bridges and major transport arteries, transformed the area. By the time the Corporation was wound up in 1992, 2,660 new businesses had set up in the city, providing 80,000 new jobs for a population that had increased four-fold to 160,000 – the fastest-growing urban area in the UK.

People were now able to drive from their 45,000 new houses on twenty-one new major grid-roads crossing the city, cycle along 230km (150 miles) of safely segregated new Redways, spend leisure time in 4,000 acres of new protected parkland – 20 per cent of the city area – and consequently experience a 30 per cent increase in new wildlife attracted, in part, by the 20 million trees and shrubs that had been planted for the new city.

Milton Keynes Council currently oversees the services for around 250,000 people. Residents enjoy not only many protected characteristics of the original villages and towns but also a unique heritage going back some 150 million years. Invading Saxons, Romans, Vikings, Danes and Normans – the 'foreign' ancestors of many 'natives' of Milton Keynes – all chose to settle in the area. From dinosaurs, prehistoric hunters and settlers, through the various invaders, to pioneers of stagecoach, canal, railway, road and motorway travel – Milton Keynes is a precious microcosm of English history.

By 2031, Milton Keynes will be the nation's tenth largest urban area, with around 350,000 people. Now, as we enter its latest expansion phase, this book is offered as a celebration of the unique character not only of the new city area, but also of its citizens who have invested their energies and futures in an exceptional venture.

PREHISTORY AT
CALDECOTTE LAKE

CALDECOTTE LAKE'S ICHTHYOSAURUS. 150 million years ago, Milton Keynes' first known resident swam around in what is now called Caldecotte Lake. His huge eyes, elongated mouth and sharp teeth, his four-metre (13ft) length, his dolphin-like fins and streamlined shape all made him a fearsome and most effective hunter. Fish, octopus and mammals unfortunate enough to be swimming too close met a swift end in his massive jaws. He was the mighty Fish Lizard, or ichthyosaurus. His remains gradually converted into fossilised rock, and in 1982 he surfaced again, unearthed by construction workers digging foundations for the new city of Milton Keynes.

CALDECOTTE LAKE TODAY. Now, new city residents pursue somewhat different 'prey' here. Called locally 'three-mile lake' – one of the largest lakes in Milton Keynes, constructed to control floods from the River Ouzel – Caldecotte hosts many outdoor adventure activities: sailing, canoeing and kayaking, climbing and archery, and even orienteering, fencing and bushcraft. For quieter moments, a Redway cycle path and footpath circle the lake – past bird-watching hides. Here, a rare visitor might be seen, like the first-ever Buckinghamshire-recorded Spotted Sandpiper from North America (May 2011) or the Great Northern Diver which, like the ichthyosaurus before it, hunts fish. (*Photograph courtesy of Andy Sutton, The Parks Trust*)

ANCIENT FLOODS OF THE RIVER GREAT OUSE

HAVERSHAM BRIDGE, WOLVERTON. Many parts of the new city area anciently suffered from poor drainage resulting from a thick layer of boulder clay. If people were to thrive here, they had to master the land. The first attempts occurred around 2,500 BC with the New Stone-Age (or Neolithic) farming communities. At Stacey Bushes, Westbury Farm and Heelands, for example, there is evidence of early settlers having dug banana-shaped pits for drainage sumps. But the River Great Ouse could rise 3.5m (11ft) above normal – as it did here at Haversham Bridge in 1939, destroying a bridge constructed only eighteen months before to replace one battered by earlier floods!
(Photograph courtesy of Living Archive)

HAVERSHAM BRIDGE TODAY. Now, bordering the Ouse Valley Park, Haversham Bridge is
protected from the vagaries of the river. Since the mid-1970s, the built areas of Bletchley,
Stony Stratford, Wolverton, New Bradwell, Loughton and Simpson have avoided frequent
and destructive flooding. A complex drainage system city-wide includes eleven 'balancing
lakes' designed as storm-water storage reservoirs, such as at Caldecotte, Willen, Tongwell,
and Furzton. As one of the many parks and open spaces maintained by the Parks Trust, Ouse
Valley Park also re-creates habitats cleared by early farmers 3,000 years ago, with its ancient
mills and modern floodplain forests.
(Photograph courtesy of Bob Hill)

FROM IRON AGE TO BOAT BASIN AT PENNYLAND

FARMTRACK TOWARDS PENNYLAND, 1971. A stone-age hunter dropped his flint axe around here some 10,000 years ago. Like his contemporaries who lost their flint weapons in Loughton Valley and Fenny Stratford, he was not a settler. They all survived only by moving on, hunting and fishing around the marshes of the Great Ouse and Ouzel rivers. However, around 1200 BC, 'Iron Age' people were settling throughout the area in Little Woolstone, Fenny, Westcroft, Woughton, Downs Barn, Blue Bridge and Pennyland. Their stronger iron

tools facilitated efficient farming which combined
cereal crops with stock-rearing. Their small villages
of a single extended family were enclosed by a ditch –
possibly flood control.
*(Photograph courtesy of Iain Cawthorne Collection,
Living Archive)*

PENNYLAND BOAT BASIN, 2012. This view typifies
how the new city has exploited another milestone of
its history. The canal threading its way through Milton
Keynes was originally the longest and widest ever
built in Britain by one company – the Grand Junction,
officially opened in 1805. The thirteen canal bridges
then built between Fenny and Stony increased threefold
under new city development; and two new boat basins
were created, at Milton Keynes Marina (1986), and
at Pennyland (1983-4). Cited as an example of good
practice with high quality design, the Pennyland basin
was ingeniously constructed by means of 'cut-and-fill' –
excavated earth was deployed for the road embankment
and bridge over the canal.
(Photograph courtesy of Bob Hill)

THE ROMAN VILLA
AT BANCROFT

ROMAN VILLA, AD 400. The city area hosted eight large estates centred on a Roman villa – in Milton Keynes Village, Stantonbury, Wymbush, Walton, Shenley Brook End, two in Bletchley and – the most extensively excavated – Bancroft. This showed evidence of under-floor central heating, sauna, steam room and massage parlour, colonnaded verandas and porch, an ornamental walled garden with fish-pond and a summer house. Residents left behind their coins (1,000 of them), their jewellery (see inset), and even an old shoe (size 7½, or 41). Nearby was a mausoleum containing the remains of three males aged thirty to fifty, one pregnant female aged eighteen to twenty-four, and four children under the age of four.
(Photograph courtesy of MKDC/CNT/EP)

BANCROFT VILLA TODAY now hosts interested visitors and community events. It forms part of the North Loughton Valley Park – maintained by the Parks Trust – along with its 'wet/dry' balancing lake, the city's famous Concrete Cows, and the Roman Park Residents' Club. Here, locals can enjoy a drink without having to brew it themselves as slaves had to in the Bancroft Roman malting oven, using home-grown barley. They don't, as slaves had to, stoke fires for cooking; they enjoy snacks or dinners in-house. Nor do they play backgammon on a Roman decorated limestone board – rather there is pool, table-tennis, darts and squash with quiz nights, karaoke nights, race nights and seasonal entertainments. (*Photograph courtesy of The Parks Trust*)

THE MEDIEVAL MARKET
SQUARE, STONY STRATFORD

MARKET SQUARE, *c*.1910. Stony Stratford received its Market Charter in 1194. Traders here sold not only local sheep and cattle, but also eels from the moated farms of Old Wolverton and Woolstone. They sold fish from the ponds of Loughton, Simpson and 'Middleton' (Milton Keynes) villages, rabbits farmed from The Warren, pigeons from the dovecotes of Bradwell Bury, and ground wheat and corn from the windmills of Great Linford and Tattenhoe – among the earliest windmills recorded in Britain. The Crown Inn (right) also served as the Lord of the Manor's courthouse; in 1777 the Methodist John Wesley preached under the elm tree (left), a ministry attracting two million followers by the 1850s.

(Photograph courtesy of the Living Archive)

MARKET SQUARE, 2012. The Square still hosts a monthly farmers' market. The weekly market ceased in the early 1900s – then, children played round the horse trough, the animal pens and beneath the boughs of Wesley's Elm. Now visitors vie for parking spaces around the new tree commemorating Wesley's visit. The Crown still plies its trade as a pub-restaurant; its last Great Court Leet and Jury was held in 1896. Built in 1666 as a coaching stop, the inn still shows where coach-drivers tethered their horses. The shop (centre) continues a centuries-old tradition of trading. The early picture shows an ironmonger's; the modern one is Cox & Robinson's, one of Stony's oldest established firms.
(Photograph courtesy of Bob Hill)

SEVENTEENTH-CENTURY MANOR HOUSE, GREAT LINFORD

GREAT LINFORD MANOR is pictured here in 1979, when the house and grounds look somewhat neglected. Successor to the Roman villa, a manor was the headquarters for the 'Squire', a property-owner second in status only to the peerage; and his manor house was the

most splendid residence in the neighbourhood. Completed in 1680 by the Lord Mayor of London Sir William Pritchard, Great Linford Manor House joined an impressive line of grand residences in the city area – at Loughton, Water Hall, Woughton, Walton and Willen. Sir William added to his country seat a schoolroom, a schoolmaster's house and six almshouses, each containing one room with a fireplace, cupboard, washstand and outside privy – all in use until the 1960s.
(Photograph courtesy of MKDC/CNT/EP archive)

LINFORD MANOR PARK, 2011. The park surrounding the house is run by The Parks Trust. The schoolroom and almshouses are now Community Arts Workshops with the two pavilions (stables that look like houses) used as studios and meeting rooms. The water gardens are a popular picnicking area. One had been destroyed when the Grand Junction Canal was cut through the estate and another lies hidden in the trees. Linford Manor Park hosts the Waterside Festival every June – one of the city's biggest events, featuring live music, boat rides, open studios, stalls, dance and crafts. The Manor House was converted to residential recording studios in 1984 – still its main function – by producer Harry Maloney.
(Photograph courtesy of Bob Hill)

17

FROM CLASSICAL HERITAGE
TO HOSPICE CARE

ST MARY MAGDALENE, 1970s. Willen's famous church was designed by Robert Hooke (1635-1703), colleague of Christopher Wren's, curator of the Royal Society and a leading scientist of his day. The builder Richard Atterbury, who also constructed the Great Linford Almshouses, installed the pews, reading desk and pulpit that are used today. The project cost

£5,000 in 1680. Willen's Lord of the Manor, Richard Busby, was headmaster of Westminster School. On his death in 1695, the Busby Trust managed the estate for charitable purposes until 1948. This, and the fact that a hospice was recorded nearby in medieval times, seem appropriate credentials for the evolution of one of the city's most popular charities.
(*Photograph courtesy of Living Archive*)

WILLEN HOSPICE, 2012. Massive efforts by volunteers and donors enabled a new city hospice to open its doors in 1981, when Willen Manor House became its home. The garden provided vegetables, fruit and eggs; community events, jumble sales, sponsorships and city hospice shops swelled the coffers. Many celebrities visited, including Diana, Princess of Wales. The Hospice Lottery, the MK Midnight Moo walks, parachute jumps and countless charity runs have helped fund running costs of £4 million a year. The hospice is now assisted by over 700 volunteers, has 10 shops and 20 in-patient beds. Caring for around 600 patients a year, it still relies on donations, with specialist palliative care free to all.
(*Photograph courtesy of Bob Hill*)

FROM FLOOD CONTROL
TO WATER SPORTS

WILLEN LAKE CONSTRUCTION, *c.*1973. To prevent the age-old problem of flooding in the city area – an area 7 miles long and 8 miles wide – 'balancing lakes' were constructed as storm-water storage reservoirs. They hold excess rainwater until the deluge has abated and the city's swollen rivers (Great Ouse, Ouzel and Loughton Brook) have subsided. The

lakes are automatically adjusted at Cotton Valley
Control Centre. Forming a protective girdle around
the city are Tongwell Lake in the north; Brickkiln
reservoir near Stony, Bradwell reservoir, Lodge
Lake and Loughton Reservoir in the west; Furzton
Reservoir, Mount Farm Lake, Simpson Reservoir and
Caldecotte Lake in the south; and Walton Lake and
Willen Lake in the east.
(Photograph courtesy of MKDC/CNT/EP archive)

WILLEN LAKE, 2005. Willen Lake is visited
by a million people a year. On the south lake
they windsurf, canoe, water-ski, go yachting or
power-boating – or, as here, compete in the annual
Dragon Boat Festival, with many of the contestants
raising money for charity. On the north lake, they
walk, cycle, fish or birdwatch – where observers
have recorded over 200 species. The inaccessible
island here makes it an ideal sanctuary for nesting
water birds not usually seen in urban areas, such
as herons and terns. Birds circle the Willen Peace
Pagoda, perch on Willen's stone circle, soar around
the sought-after lakeside business premises or crowd
hopefully on the lakeshore for food.
(Photograph courtesy of The Parks Trust)

THE STAGECOACH ERA

SWAN HOTEL, *c*.1920. Rebuilt in 1879 on the site of a fourteenth-century inn, the Swan served a major route through England that was over 1,000 years old. The London-Chester Watling Street crossed Fenny or 'the ford' ½ mile from the Roman camp Magiovinium. The Swan's alehouse and stables became an early service station. In the seventeenth and eighteenth centuries around thirty such staging-posts traded on Watling Street in the Milton Keynes area. By 1800, with 35 coaches and 350 animals using the route a day, turnpikes at Fenny, Stony and Two Mile Ash charged a halfpenny for a pack-horse and a shilling for a coach to contribute to its upkeep.
(Photograph courtesy of Living Archive)

SWAN HOTEL, 2012. The inn still trades at the junction of Watling Street, Aylesbury Road (left) and Simpson Road, but its custom comes not so much from travellers using the A5 as the main north-south route through England: the M1 motorway and West Coast railway line are the modern thoroughfares. Rather it has local trade, along with football fans gathering for the match at the nearby Stadium:mk – home of the Milton Keynes Dons. One visiting fan reported: 'It has a basic range of beers but they serve good value food on a match day... and a fantastic breakfast until 1.30 p.m.!'
(Photograph courtesy of Bob Hill)

ARRIVAL OF THE CANAL – THE GRAND UNION, FENNY STRATFORD

FENNY STRATFORD, *c.*1900. In 1792, the plan for the new 90-mile Grand Junction Canal was discussed at The Bull, Stony Stratford. Engineer John Barnes and local worthies including the Marquis of Buckingham agreed to build the canal from Braunston to Brentford passing through Fenny Stratford, Simpson, Woughton, the Woolstones, Great Linford and Wolverton.

Some remarkable constructions are at Fenny: its basin and dock (1800), a unique pump house (1840), and 'Lock 22' – not only the shallowest lock on the canal (just 30cm) but also the only one with a swing bridge across the lock chamber.
(*Photography courtesy of Living Archive*)

FENNY CANAL PATH, 2009. Competing railways and burgeoning road transport marked the decline of the Grand Junction Canal by the 1920s. In January 1929, it was amalgamated with other canals into a combined waterway, the Grand Union Canal; in January 1963, it came under control of the new, nationalised British Waterways Board. Four years later, the designation of Milton Keynes gave rise to the claim that the new city had 'more canal miles than Venice!' The city's 150-mile cycle network, the Redways, includes the twelve miles of the Grand Union Canal towpaths which enable cyclists to access city landmarks like the National Bowl, the Teardrop Lakes – and the famous Concrete Cows.
(*Photograph courtesy of Bob Hill*)

THE IRON TRUNK, CANAL AQUEDUCT, OLD WOLVERTON

THE IRON TRUNK, *c.*1920. William Jessup's Iron Trunk Aqueduct at Wolverton (1810) is a Scheduled Ancient Monument. At 30m (100 feet) long, it is as wide as the River Great Ouse that it spans (5m-16ft). Flanked by 'cattle creep' tunnels (to allow animals through to pasture), it keeps the canal 10m (35ft) above the river, obviating the need for nine locks. Known as the 'ackidoc' to locals, it was built by Reynolds & Co. of Ketley, Shropshire at a cost of £3,667. Live sheep from Northampton and Grenadier Guards from Liverpool were among the first to travel on the canal direct to London. *(Photograph courtesy of Living Archive, Baz Green)*

THE AQUEDUCT, 2012. The Iron Trunk in its modern setting of the Ouse Valley Park is now peopled by walkers, nature-lovers, cyclists and narrow-boat tourists. In addition, it has a successor to rival Jessup's and Reynolds' considerable accomplishments. In 1991 MKDC built a new £4 million aqueduct over the grid-road V6 Grafton Street for the canal. Four times as long as the Iron Trunk (120m), it was the first to be built in the nation for half a century – with not only a towpath but, incorporated with it, the celebrated city-wide Milton Keynes Redway cycling system.

(Photograph courtesy of Bob Hill)

A NEW CITY CANAL
BRIDGE FOR H5 PORTWAY

BRIDGE CONSTRUCTION, 1986. Portway was known to medieval travellers 750 years ago. It was a track from Newport Pagnell accessing the markets of Fenny and Stony Stratford. When the canal arrived in the early 1800s, thirteen bridges were constructed in the city area for such tracks. 180 years later, MKDC created another twenty-three – specifically to withstand

the robust needs of modern traffic and incorporated into the unique grid-road system designed for the city. The grid-roads running north-south (vertically on the map) were called 'streets' prefixed with 'V'; those running east-west (horizontally) were called 'ways' with the prefix 'H'. The H5 Portway was one of the earliest, and most important, roads for the new city.

(Photograph courtesy of Living Archive)

UNDER H5 PORTWAY, 2012. H5 Portway starts 1½ miles east of here at Northfield Roundabout, where it joins with H6, Childs Way, for M1 Junction 14. These two are the main horizontal arteries of Central Milton Keynes, enclosing between them the city's central areas as they travel west: Willen South Lake, Campbell Park, CMK shopping and business centres, and MK Central Railway station. This modern view of the Redway path alongside the canal and its waterside homes belies the nature of the bridge above: a busy dual carriageway just five minutes from the city centre.

(Photograph courtesy of Bob Hill)

FROM FARMLAND TO CENTRAL MILTON KEYNES

THE CMK SITE, 1971. A farmer said of this land: 'It was in a terrible condition with "twitches" (couch grass) and masses of anthills...' With an otherwise empty site, MKDC designers and architects of Central Milton Keynes were at pains to make it right: 'CMK was designed in a totality.... The idea was to make the public domain of such a high quality, so simple and plain

that it would survive whatever came and went around it'. The main Shopping Building would be flanked by tree-lined boulevards leading to Milton Keynes Central railway station at the west end and Campbell Park at the east.
(Photograph courtesy of the Iain Cawthorne Collection, Living Archive)

CMK CRICKET, 2012. At the city's heart, Campbell Park hosts many major festivals and events – May Day Festival, World Picnic, City Spectacular, Fireworks Display, and open-air film and theatre. It accommodates an imaginative mix of formal gardens, water features, woodland and open pasture – where sheep graze year-round, so close to a city centre. The Belvedere, created from CMK building spoil, provides unrivalled views. Nearby is a memorial to Lord Campbell of Eskan, MKDC's first chairman and the first Freeman of the City: 'If you seek his memorial, look around'. The cricket pitch here attracts county, league and national sides, as well as spectators who enjoy the matches for free.
(Photograph courtesy of Pete Norton, The Parks Trust)

31

THE STEAM RAILWAY AGE

ENGINEERING WOLVERTON'S RAILWAY. Whilst farming was still a major occupation at the new city's birth, canals had been superseded by the railways. In 1831 George Stephenson, inventor of the world's first steam engine, *The Rocket*, initiated the idea of a 'permanent way' between London and Birmingham. The project started in 1833. By 1838, a year after Queen Victoria's coronation, his son Robert had engineered 112 miles of it. This included Wolverton's 1½ mile-long embankment – with its viaduct of six blue-brick arches 17.3m (57ft) high, and a span of 18.2m (60ft) carrying the railway line for 201m (660ft) over the River Great Ouse.
(Building the Embankment c.1835 and the Viaduct c.1900, photograph courtesy of Living Archive)

THE VIADUCT, 2011. Viewed from the Ouse Valley Park, Wolverton's embankment and viaduct today carry West Coast Mainline trains from London to the West Midlands, the North West, North Wales, and Central Scotland – the busiest mixed-traffic railway route in Britain. Fast 125mph intercity trains and suburban commuter trains provide around 75 million passenger journeys a year on the line, most of them passing through Milton Keynes. It is also one of the busiest freight routes in Europe – carrying 43 per cent of all UK rail freight traffic. As engines variously race or trundle across the viaduct, the River Great Ouse still meanders beneath, not just through farmland now, but through parkland meadows.
(Photograph courtesy of Bob Hill)

THE WORLD-FAMOUS
WOLVERTON WORKS

WOLVERTON WORKS WORKSHOP, *c*.1910. Described
even in 1844 as 'gigantic... one of the wonders of modern
times', the railway works became the largest single
employer in North Bucks – an engine driver earning
four times more than an agricultural labourer. In 1906
Wolverton Works was at its zenith, covering 80 acres and
employing nearly 5,000 people. It was internationally
renowned in industrial development: its Power House
was the first in the UK to be completely lit and powered
electrically; and Wolverton-trained railway fitters,
coach-body makers and track maintenance men were
in demand all over the world, including South Africa,
Australia, Asia and the Americas. It was the largest works
in the UK solely devoted to carriage building and repair.
(Photograph courtesy of Living Archive)

NEW WOLVERTON WORKSHOP, 2009. By the 1960s, the Works had changed from a world-famous 'engineering laboratory', employing thousands, to that of a repair shop and depot with a few hundred employees. However, at 174 years old (in 2012) it is the oldest continuously functioning railway factory in Britain, possibly in the world. The Works were privatised first through BREL and sold on to Alstom. Subsequently Railcare, which was formed in 2007, bought the business and now operates the site as a 'total Rolling Stock solution... vehicle and component overhaul with incident repair, spares and logistics'. The company received the 2010 'Excellence in People Development Award' from the MK Chamber of Commerce.
(Photograph courtesy of Bob Hill)

RAILWAY HOUSES, WOLVERTON

THE LITTLE STREETS, *c.*1920. Railway workers brought their families to Wolverton from all over the country: birth-places ranged from London to Scotland, from Cumberland, Lancashire and Birmingham, to Wales, Essex and Cornwall. The railway company built for them the world's first self-sufficient new town, complete with customised facilities for health, education, places of worship and even pubs. In 1840, eighty-four terraced railway houses were ready for occupation in 'the little streets' – including Ledsam Street, shown here – around Glynn Square. This model for a Victorian grid-pattern housing development was soon adopted throughout Wolverton and New Bradwell, eerily prescient of new city infrastructure. *(Photograph courtesy of Living Archive)*

WOLVERTON PARK, 2012. Opposite the 'little streets' – demolished in the early 1960s – was a vast recreation ground which the railway company opened in 1885 in front of 16,000 excited residents. Each year after, the Wolverton Park celebration included processions, bands, cycle races, athletes, footballers, tennis players; and, in the evening, dancing and fireworks. From 1887, the park hosted Wolverton Football Club, which became one of the country's leading teams, playing Tottenham and Chelsea. Today the site has been redeveloped for 300 homes. Yet its railway heritage lives on: some of the apartments are in the converted Royal Train Shed and the Carriage Works (right). The scheme has won six major awards since 2008. *(Photograph courtesy of Bob Hill)*

THE RAILWAY
AT BLETCHLEY

BLETCHLEY RAILWAY STATION, *c*.1940. Bletchley
Station was built in 1847, following the opening of the
line to Bedford linking Oxford with Cambridge – the
'Varsity Line'. By 1852, 100 men were employed in
three acres of sidings and sheds at Bletchley, handling
seventy steam trains a day. The station had its stone
entrance roofed so that horse-drawn taxis could deposit
their customers under shelter. Outside were tea-rooms
and later a coffee tavern, well patronised by railway
employees and travellers. One local story is that Winston
Churchill would be seen at the station, apparently going
into the platform air-raid shelter, but actually accessing
nearby Bletchley Park – the secret code-breaking
'Station X' – via an underground passage.
(*Photograph courtesy of Living Archive*)

BLETCHLEY STATION, 2012. Bletchley was for a time an intercity station, but its role passed to the new Milton Keynes Central Station in 1982. The east-west route was downgraded, taking Bletchley's importance as a junction with it. The old station building was demolished; its utilitarian replacement with a rather bleak forecourt had a new type of ticket control office, new waiting room and bookstall. Currently, the station's facilities include cycle storage, a coffee bar and over 600 car parking spaces. However, there is a possibility that the station will again host the through-link from either Oxford or Bedford to Milton Keynes – with hopefully attendant improved development.
(Photograph courtesy of Bob Hill)

STACEY HILL – FROM VICTORIAN FARMHOUSE TO CITY MUSEUM

STACEY HILL FARMHOUSE, 1971. Built in 1847 as a model farm, Stacey Hill near Wolverton was part of the Radcliffe Trust estate, let to tenant farmers until the new city arrived. Before the Second World War, the farm hosted the National Cross Country Championships, the oldest

event of its kind in the world; and the spectacular Air Pageant was held there, supporting pre-NHS hospital funds. As part of its community remit, MKDC set up the farmhouse as a continuing social amenity. Writers and artists-in-residence worked there, including Liz Leyh, who created the Concrete Cows. In 1972, the Stacey Hill Collection of Industrial and Rural Life was also founded, forerunner of Milton Keynes Museum.
(Photograph courtesy of the Iain Cawthorne Collection, Living Archive)

THE STEAM PLOUGH (Bill Griffiths, MKM director, is left of the picture). As items were retrieved from farms and factories closing down to make way for the city, the new museum became a repository of unique and amazing artefacts. One was this invention from a tenant farmer at Woughton and Linford Lodge, William Smith. In 1855, inspired by the steam age, he patented his 'Steam Subsoiler'. He claimed it disturbed little soil and produced better tilth, unlike the horse-drawn plough. By 1862 he had 200 customers, but in 1877, in a fit of pique with local trade unionists, he bricked up the machinery in his barn – where it stayed until its discovery eight decades later, in 1958!
(Photograph courtesy of Milton Keynes Museum)

THE STEAM TRAM IN STONY STRATFORD

THE STEAM TRAM, *c*.1920. One facility provided for
Wolverton Works employees was the tramway, which
opened in 1887 and ran between the Barleymow pub
in Stony Stratford and Wolverton Station. Its tram cars
were the largest in the world, holding 100 passengers
apiece; and they were pulled along by the 'Puffing Billy'
steam engine on a narrow-gauge railway in the middle
of Stratford Road. Beforehand, most of its 700 daily
passengers had to walk from Stony to Wolverton and back
again. Fares cost a shilling a week, but it saved in shoe
leather – boots were as much as seven shillings a pair,
nearly a third of a week's pay.
(Photograph courtesy of Living Archive)

THE SAME SITE, 2011. The steam tram was the last to operate in Britain, and one of the few to run on rural routes. Successive companies that took over the enterprise faced financial difficulties and strong competition from the buses. Tram staff joined the General Strike in May 1926; the tram way never opened again. The rails were taken up in the same year. Milton Keynes Museum now houses one of the two original 100-seater double-decker cars, 44ft (13m) long and extensively refurbished – as well as a large single-decker car. There is also a section of the original track, rescued from the mud during construction of the Stony Stratford by-pass.

(Photograph courtesy of Bob Hill)

HAYES, STEAM AND MOTOR BOAT BUILDERS OF STONY STRATFORD

THE PAT TUGBOAT, *c*.1920. Edward Hayes (1818-77), originally apprenticed at Wolverton Works, set up a business in agricultural engineering employing sixty mechanics. His son Edward (1845-1917) specialised in building boats on the site of the present London Road garage. As this

was some distance from the canal, a steam traction engine had to haul the finished boat – 70ft (23m) long – along Stony High Street to Old Stratford. Hayes' steam launches became famous: they could tow 500 tons at 11mph. One of the Hayes apprentices in the 1890s was Sir Frederick Rebbeck, KBE, who helped design the *Titanic* in 1911. (*Photograph courtesy of Living Archive*)

THE RESCUED TUGBOAT, 2012. Renamed *The Wey* in the 1930s, the *Pat* is the last known Hayes motor tug boat, preserved for the city. 'Hayes' Boatyard, Watling Works' closed in 1925 after sixty-five years building boats for Britain, France, Russia and Egypt. Built in 1924, this survivor was the last of 300 vessels built at the yard. She spent her working life on the Thames, once being used to break ice on the frozen river. Donated by the Environment Agency, transported by CMG Rescue Services, supported by Milton Keynes Community Foundation and Stony Stratford Town Council, she found her final resting place at Milton Keynes Museum.
(*Photograph courtesy of Bob Hill*)

EARLY MOTOR BUS SERVICES, STONY STRATFORD

MOTOR TRAM, c.1920s. The nation's first motor bus services began after the Highways Act of 1898. Many towns from Bradford to Clacton all claimed to have the earliest – as did the motor bus company which introduced a bus service between Newport Pagnell and Olney in 1898. In 1921, the United Counties Omnibus Co. was incorporated with a major shareholder

(Tillings) having strong links in Stony Stratford. The motor tram shown here in Stony High Street is probably one of theirs. The shop behind it, Calladine and Son, was owned by a town worthy who enabled the creation in the same year of the Stony Stratford Sports Ground.
(Photograph courtesy of Living Archive)

SAME VIEW, 2012. United Counties' fleet of 150 local buses in Bucks and Northants had expanded by 1933 with long-distance coaches travelling to Torquay, Oxford and London. Nationalisation in 1948 brought major expansion, doubling the fleet to 500 vehicles. Towards the end of the 1970s, the company had developed a major maintenance and vehicle depot in the new city, at Winterhill. After privatisation and deregulation, however, the company was split up, its rump being purchased by Stagecoach in 1987. Currently, Milton Keynes has one of the busiest coach stations in the country – the new Coachway having recently been opened near Junction 14.
(Photograph courtesy of Bob Hill)

FROM BRICKWORKS TO
NATURE RESERVE

BLETCHLEY BRICKWORKS, *c*.1950. For over 200 years, independent brickyards flourished in the Milton Keynes city area. The earliest recorded was in Denbigh (Bailey's, 1700). Situated on a rich seam of blue clay deposits, more than twenty small companies proliferated, serving the burgeoning canal and railway industries with bricks for houses, bridges, tunnels, locks, stations and factories. By the 1930s, however, all the independent brickyards had been superseded by three large companies. One, London Brick Co., was the largest brick-making company in England and the second biggest employer in Bletchley, with around 400 men making 4½ million bricks a week.
(Photograph courtesy of Living Archive)

THE BLUE LAGOON, 2010. By the late 1970s, the brickworks had ceased production with its hundreds of workers dispersed. Its labour-intensive process, the hot and dusty conditions, the dominance of its high brick-kiln chimneys – all had had their day. Steel, concrete and glass were deemed more suited to modern buildings. MKDC remodelled the site in the late 1980s to

create the Borough's only local nature reserve. It covers 75 acres with two lakes and a mix of trees, scrub, long grass and downs. Visited by birdwatchers, butterfly enthusiasts, anglers and divers – the latter using sunken vehicles for exploration – the 18m-deep Blue Lagoon supports a diverse eco-system.

(Photograph courtesy of Bob Hill)

McCORQUODALE'S – VICTORIAN PRINTERS TO TWENTY-FIRST-CENTURY HOMES

MCCORQUODALE'S COMPOSING ROOM, *c*.1905. George McCorquodale opened his first factory in Wolverton in 1878 at the behest of his friend, the LNW chairman Sir Richard Moon. The railway town had plenty of work for its men, but their daughters had few

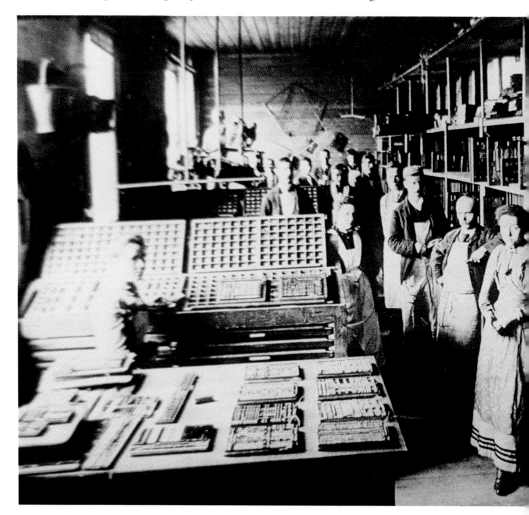

opportunities. By 1886, the factory employed 120 women and 20 men – producing envelopes, books, forms and commercial stationery. Girls started work at thirteen or fourteen years old and were employed until they married. They worked a fifty-four-hour week, starting at 6 a.m. (with a half-day on Saturday). They were provided with dining, reading and recreation rooms; pension funds paid for holidays; and they were given service bonuses.
(Photograph courtesy of Living Archive)

THE MCCORQUODALE BUILDING, 2012. The printing works dominated the west end of Stratford Road and developed throughout most of the twentieth century, having secured Government contracts for postal stamps, stationery, old-age pension and other benefit forms. Football pools massively increased print runs on postal orders, ensuring that the firm remained profitable. However, the arrival of the digital age, management changes and several takeovers meant that, by the 1990s, the buildings were deemed obsolete. The company headquarters moved away and the land was used for homes, though still retaining the façade of one of the buildings, dated 1912.
(Photograph courtesy of Bob Hill)

ARMY RECRUITS – FROM THE FIRST WORLD WAR TO AFGHANISTAN.

ARMY RECRUITS, WOLVERTON, 1914. In 1913 army manoeuvres centred on the Wolverton area – with 40,000 men, 15,000 horses, and countless carts and motor-vehicles. Young men were entranced by the bands, the uniforms and the weapons; young women by the host of young men. Even King George V visited to see it all. When war broke out on 4 August 1914, Wolverton men volunteered in droves. 'The scene at the station beggared description. Nothing like it had been known to Wolverton... The band played patriotic tunes and the people of

Wolverton showed a spirit of patriotism which in every British heart will give the Germans the time of their lives.' *Wolverton Express, 7 August 1914*
(Photograph courtesy of Living Archive)

TERRITORIAL ARMY, CMK. Nine decades later, the Mayor of Milton Keynes, Cllr Jan Lloyd, inspects local Territorial Army soldiers from 7th Battalion The Rifles following the regiment's Freedom Parade in city centre – the greatest honour a civic authority can bestow. Later, 7 Rifles E Company's city barracks in Blakelands were officially renamed 'The John Howard Barracks' commemorating the famous commander from the local Oxfordshire and Buckinghamshire Light Infantry – an antecedent of The Rifles. Howard, who seized strategically critical Normandy bridges on the eve of D-Day 1944, was immortalised in the film *The Longest Day*. Formed in 2007, The Rifles is the largest regiment of the British Army, involved in combat operations in Iraq and Afghanistan.
(Photograph courtesy of 7 Rifles E Company)

BLETCHLEY PARK – THE NATION'S SECRET SECOND WORLD WAR WEAPON

BLETCHLEY PARK STAFF, *c.*1910. From 1882 until 1937, Bletchley Park was home to Sir Herbert and Lady Leon. They hosted the famous Bletchley Show, several Liberal Party rallies, even royal hunts. An army of staff maintained their 44 acres of parkland and 27-bedroom mansion. Up to 200 staff were employed at Bletchley Park in its heyday – grooms, gardeners, engineers, plumbers,

carpenters, and house-servants supervised by the butler and housekeeper. They oversaw facilities enjoyed only by the rich – nickel-plated baths, marble-topped lavatories and heated towel rails; oak-panelled reception rooms with central heating and electric lights powered from their own generator; even a laundry. *(Photograph courtesy of Living Archive)*

BLETCHLEY PARK, 2012. Acquired by the Government's top-secret agency GCHQ in 1939, 'Station X' became the stuff of legend. Bletchley Park was where code-breakers cracked Germany's supposedly unbreakable Enigma codes, arguably shortening the war by at least two years. It later housed a Teachers' Training College, the Diplomatic Wireless Service, the Ministry of Aviation, and British Telecom. Now an intrinsic part of Milton Keynes, it is run by a Trust dedicated to preserving its pioneering wartime importance in computerised code-breaking. Its success was through geniuses like the mathematician Alan Turing and the novelist Angus Wilson; and, as Winston Churchill said, through the anonymous thousands of 'geese who laid the golden egg and never cackled.' *(Photograph courtesy of Bob Hill)*

BLETCHLEY
LEISURE CENTRE

BLETCHLEY LEISURE CENTRE, 1974. Bletchley's first Leisure Centre replaced the outdoor
Queens Pool and the gardens around it – 'one of the nicest parts of Bletchley' said one local.
'We all thought it was terrible when the Leisure Centre was built over them.' The architects
for the new centre – Faulkner Brown-Hendy-Watkinson – created what became iconic
city structures: a transparent pyramid housing the Leisure Pool, and a curving walkway

overlooking reflection pools. In 1976, the third World Kendo Championships were held in the main sports hall; from 1980, as the Jennie Lee Theatre, it hosted performances from such as the Royal Shakespeare Company, Billy Connolly and Showaddywaddy.
(Photograph courtesy of MKDC/CNT/EP archive)

NEW LEISURE CENTRE, 2012. Some people tried to get the pyramid building listed to prevent demolition but the site was cleared for housing and a new multi-storey car-park. The adjacent new centre is now home to a health club which includes a fitness studio with high-tech machines, a dance studio, pedal studio, sauna and steam room. It also has a 25m pool – not the 'leisure pool' of the old pyramid – badminton and squash courts and seven indoor bowls rinks. The multi-purpose sports hall no longer has to double up as a drama or entertainments centre: Milton Keynes Theatre opened in the city centre in 1999.
(Photograph courtesy of Bob Hill)

A HOSPITAL
FOR MILTON
KEYNES

HOSPITAL SITE, 1971. Local people lobbied for
a hospital for years. A Hospital Action Group
campaigned with the slogan 'Milton Keynes is dying
for a hospital!' and placed a giant orange question
mark on a grid-road near the proposed site. When
building was postponed to 1980, protesters bombarded
the House of Commons, handing in a petition signed
by 18,000 people to the Under-Secretary for Health,
Dr David Owen. Although a small Community Hospital
started at Eaglestone in 1979, Milton Keynes Hospital
was finally opened on this site in 1984.
*(Photograph courtesy of The Iain Cawthorne Collection,
Living Archive)*

MILTON KEYNES HOSPITAL, 2012. The new hospital opened with around 300 beds when
the city's population was 115,000. By the time the hospital celebrated its 25th anniversary in
2009, there were over 560 beds for the borough's then population of 240,000. Its cohort of
1,000 staff had increased to 3,000, with 500 volunteers helping deliver care to patients. There
are now 300,000 patients a year, 20,000 of whom are admitted, and around 4,000 more are
new-born. Its 60-hectare site includes a Postgraduate Education centre; an Oncology and Cancer
Unit funded by the Macmillan Cancer Charity; a sixty-bed Day Surgery Treatment Centre; and a
wide–ranging arts collection curated by MK Arts For Health.
(Photograph courtesy of Bob Hill)

ANCIENT CHURCH
AND MODERN PAGODA

STANTON ST PETERS. This twelfth-century church (inset 1905) ceased to function after the New Bradwell church of St James was built for the new community of railway families in 1857. However, when it was discovered in 1909 that the new church had not yet been licensed for weddings, old Stanton St Peters came back temporarily into use – such as for this wedding procession. It had a Jacobean oak pulpit and altar rails, a stone bench and Norman doorway. But the church fell into disrepair; the roof collapsed in 1956. Now just a grass-covered mound of stones, it may be accessed – as then – only by an ancient track from the Black Horse bridge at Great Linford.
(Photographs courtesy of Living Archive)

WILLEN PEACE PAGODA, 1981. Milton Keynes was the first in the West to build a Peace Pagoda, in 1979. At the Foundation Ceremony in 1981, a richly draped elephant headed the procession of vividly robed Buddhist monks, accompanied by the release of thousands of white birds. Part of the international movement of the Nipponzan Myohoji Order of Buddhist monks, the Pagoda's function is 'to remind people of the need to seek world peace and peaceful means to resolve arguments'. Nearby are 1,000 cherry trees and cedars, a gift from Japan, commemorating the victims of all wars; and a temple run by Buddhist monks and nuns working to underline the importance of seeking peace in world affairs. *(Photograph courtesy of MKDC/CNT/EP archive)*

FROM DOMESDAY VILLAGE
TO EXPANSION AREA

BROUGHTON VILLAGE, *c.*1970. 'Brotone' was originally a Saxon settlement ('tun') on a brook (broc). As Broughton, it was one of eighteen city area communities of the 1086 Domesday Book and one of thirteen surviving villages by the time the new city was designated.

It acquired some significance when its twelfth-century church of St Lawrence was discovered to contain graphic medieval images; and when its main road, linking London to the Midlands, became ever more important when the plague struck seventeenth-century Fenny Stratford on Watling Street. Broughton's London Road, now a cul-de-sac, can be seen running across the centre of the picture in parallel to the M1 motorway beyond it.

(Photograph courtesy of Living Archive)

BROUGHTON COMMUNITY EVENT, 2011. Community Mobilisers work with local people to help stimulate activities and activate ideas – such as with a group of volunteers called ROAR - Resident's Opinions Achieving Results. By 2022, 4,000 families will have settled in the Eastern Expansion area of Broughton Gate and Brooklands to share community and sports facilities, play areas, health facilities, shops, allotments, primary schools, 80 hectares of employment land and a hotel. All will be protected from the motorway by a high landscaped ridge, part of the Parks Trust's network of open spaces and wildlife reserves. The picture shows part of the old village (right), some new houses and the site of Broughton Community and Sports Pavilion.

(Photograph courtesy of Community Action MK)

FROM SIDINGS TO
CITY RAILWAY STATION

CITY STATION SITE, 1974. One local remembers, 'The workman's train went down at 7.12 in the morning – eight coaches for Wolverton Works – and stopped near where the new station is. When the train come back at night, it backed into that siding.' The original valley depth can be seen from the station footbridge to Loughton over the retaining wall. On one side is Station Square; on the other are the lower railway tracks. British Rail was initially reluctant to commit itself to a new station for Milton Keynes. It was 'a year's persistent hard work,' said MKDC's General Manager Frank Henshaw, 'but it was key to establishing CMK as a major employment centre.'
(Photograph courtesy of the Iain Cawthorne Collection, Living Archive)

MILTON KEYNES CENTRAL. The new intercity station was opened by Prince Charles in May 1982 – when he also named locomotive 86211 'The City of Milton Keynes'. This ceased operating in 1986 when it was damaged in a collision. However, the city's main station building and its plaza have had a fuller life: they were used in the film *Superman IV* as a substitute for the United Nations building; and now (2012) Station Square is being redeveloped for the thousands of people that use it every day – to accommodate more buses and taxis.

BRICK-PIT TO NATIONAL BOWL

RED BALLOON DAY, 1988. One of MKDC's six goals was to make 'efficient and imaginative use of resources'. Workers at Fletton's Brickworks near Loughton would never have believed that their old brick-pit could be converted – by judicious use of spoil to form an amphitheatre – to the 'National Bowl', where 65,000 people could enjoy open-air concerts from such stars

as David Bowie, Queen, Genesis, Michael Jackson, Status Quo and Take That. In 1989, the Bowl hosted the two-day Virat Hindu Sammelan (Great Hindu Assembly) attracting over 55,000 Hindus, the largest ever gathering outside India. In 1990, citizens released 217,000 red balloons – one of the city's early symbols – which raised £60,000 for charity and broke the European Record.
(Photograph courtesy of Living Archive)

FOO FIGHTERS, 2011. In 1992, with the closure of MKDC, the Bowl was sold to Sony/Pace, and given a massive covered stage. Hundreds of performers followed – Bruce Springstein, Guns and Roses, UB40, Bon Jovi... In 1998 a £50 million plan incorporated a Millennium Dome: Nigel Kennedy, Metallica and Marilyn Manson performed. English Partnerships bought the Bowl in 2000, and Robbie Williams, Ronan Keating, Eminem and Simply Red filled the amphitheatre. In 2006 Gaming International won the tender bid; although the number of gigs has decreased, the Bowl still proves to be a crowd-puller: around 130,000 people gathered at Milton Keynes Bowl last summer to watch the Foo Fighters.
(Photograph courtesy of Living Archive)

VICTORIAN SCHOOLING TO MODERN EDUCATION

SIMPSON SCHOOL, *c*.1910. Some of these children look reasonably happy, all dressed in their Sunday best for the photograph with their teacher and his assistants. But the twenty boys and ten girls here – aged from three to thirteen – would have all been taught in the same schoolroom, with high windows to stop them looking out and curtains to divide different groups. They wrote on slates or with scratchy ink-pens, replicating in their 'copybooks' whatever their teacher chalked on the blackboard for the 'three Rs' (reading, writing and arithmetic). Lessons consisted mostly of reciting parrot-fashion until word-perfect. If pupils 'blotted their copybook' in any way, they could expect to be caned.
(Photograph courtesy of Living Archive)

THE 'TIGERS' CLASS, 2010. In 2010, the Ofsted Inspector told these pupils that their school 'is providing you with an outstanding education. You told us that you really enjoy learning because your teachers make sure you have many exciting things to do. Inspectors agree that this is the case. We were very impressed with how everyone has their say in helping to improve the school. We enjoyed your lovely singing and saw how much progress the string and brass players had made in such a short time.' The school's success is largely due to 'the inspired and dedicated leadership' of headteacher Elizabeth Bancroft who says, 'The children are our inspiration.' No wonder they look happy!
(Photograph courtesy of Loughton Manor First School)

THE OPEN UNIVERSITY –
PIONEER TO WORLD LEADER

WALTON HALL 1969. Milton Keynes has accommodated the world's first successful distance-learning university for over forty years. Based around the classical white building of Walton Hall (centre left), the Open University was founded in 1969 on the belief that communications technology could bring high quality degree-level learning to people unable to attend campus universities. There had to be equal access for all, no entry requirements, and the capability to study in any location. Lord Crowther, its first chancellor said, 'By a very

happy chance, our only local habitation will be in the new city bearing two of the widest ranging names in the history of English thought, Milton (the poet) and Keynes (the economist).'
(Photograph courtesy of the Living Archive)

THE OPEN UNIVERSITY, 2011. The OU took its first 24,000 students in 1971. Four decades later the statistics are breathtaking: it is the biggest university in the UK; its 250,000 students are served by 7,000 tutors and 5,000 academic, support and administrative staff; with partnerships worldwide, more than 1.6 million OU students have achieved their academic goals in around 600 courses; in 2011 the OU held twenty-four degree ceremonies in fifteen different locations from Dublin to Versailles. In 2006, the then chancellor, Baroness Boothroyd, opened the East Campus (centre top) after the original occupiers of the site – De Montfort University's Milton Keynes branch – withdrew. The OU houses its central Student Services there.
(Photograph courtesy of The Open University)

FROM AMATEUR PITCH TO PROFESSIONAL STADIUM

MANOR FIELDS PITCH, *c*.1975. Bletchley Sports Football Club formed in 1914 at Bletchley Park. Renamed Bletchley Town, it moved to Manor Fields in the 1950s. A semi-professional side in the 1960s, it won the UC League twice. By 1974, the club was called Milton Keynes City Football Club, with its best-ever season in 1979-80 as County Cup Final winners. However, player Barry Lines said:

'Manor Fields wasn't the greatest pitch in the world to play on. It sloped from one end to the other and from corner to corner. It was very close to the river so it was very often under water.'
(Photograph courtesy of Living Archive)

THE STADIUM:MK. Several professional football teams showed interest in moving to Milton Keynes. Wimbledon FC directors even became MK City FC directors for a possible merger. However, the home club's season foundered in 1984-5 and the idea was abandoned. Instead, MK City FC became a thriving amateur youth football club with Wimbledon finally announcing it would become the new city's professional home team in 2001. By 2004 the new 'Dons' were playing at the city's National Hockey Stadium, moving in 2007 into the purpose-built 22,000-seater Stadium:mk, officially opened by the Queen. UEFA standards, future plans – for 45,000 capacity and a continuing venue for top rugby matches – all indicate the stadium's potential regional significance.
(Photograph courtesy of Lee Scrivens, MK Dons)

FROM NATIONAL HOCKEY STADIUM TO NETWORK RAIL HUB

NATIONAL HOCKEY STADIUM, 2006. Built in 1995 for field hockey, the new national stadium had a synthetic pitch serving both national and international matches. It hosted the sixth Men's Junior World Cup in 1997 and the Women's Qualifying Tournament for the

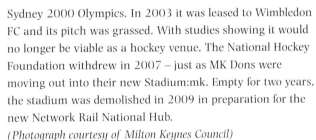

Sydney 2000 Olympics. In 2003 it was leased to Wimbledon FC and its pitch was grassed. With studies showing it would no longer be viable as a hockey venue, The National Hockey Foundation withdrew in 2007 – just as MK Dons were moving out into their new Stadium:mk. Empty for two years, the stadium was demolished in 2009 in preparation for the new Network Rail National Hub.
(Photograph courtesy of Milton Keynes Council)

THE QUADRANT, 2011. 'A key reason we chose Milton Keynes was the quality of the local talent,' said a Network Rail executive. He was referring to the keen competition among UK cities to accommodate the Quadrant, the nation's new railway hub; but in 2010 Milton Keynes won. In 2012 over 3,000 people will be working there – in Engineering, Logistics, Operations, IT, Contracts and Procurement, Planning, HR and Finance. The four main office buildings lead from a central area with facilities that include a gym, convenience store and food court – as well as environmental-friendly features such as recycled rainwater to flush toilets and electric car recharging points.
(Photograph courtesy of Bob Hill)

MILTON KEYNES' UNIQUE GRID-ROAD SYSTEM

FIRST CITY GRID-ROAD, 1970. This grid-road – H2 Millers Way – was part of the city's kilometre-square design, 'a pattern people could carry in their minds,' said Richard Llewelyn Davies, consultant for *The Plan for Milton Keynes, 1970*. A uniquely extensive and effective road system, it offered 'easy flow of traffic avoiding the congestion found in

most urban areas.' Each grid square was to have only local traffic, with higher-speed through-traffic travelling along its surrounding grid-roads. The grid-squares would also create 'zones' – of employment, residential and retail. 'People do not have to live cheek by jowl with huge distribution warehouses, noisy workshops, and busy offices and shops.' (Mark Clapson)
(Photograph courtesy of Living Archive)

GRID-ROADS AND ROUNDABOUTS. The landscaped corridors along the city's twenty-one major grid-roads and eighty-five roundabouts are managed by the Parks Trust. These 1,300 acres are considered to be 'among the outstanding features of Milton Keynes, assisting in the dispersal of many species' (MK Natural History Society). The Tree Cathedral here, at the H5 Portway/V10 Brickhill Street roundabout, has an outline based on Norwich Cathedral. Designed in 1986 by landscape architect Neil Higson, different species represent the Cathedral's sections: hornbeam and tall-growing lime for the nave, evergreens for the tower and spires, flowering fruit trees in the chapels; and springtime bulbs represent the sun shining through stained glass windows onto the ground.
(Photograph courtesy of Anne Robinson, The Parks Trust)

SNOW POWER
IN CENTRAL
MILTON KEYNES

GRID-ROAD SKIING, 1981. The Milton Keynes area,
like the rest of the nation, has been sporadically hit
by heavy snowfalls: in 1908, when Bletchley Road
(the former Queensway) was blocked; in 1947, when
blizzards buried local sheep; and in 1963, the coldest
winter since records began in 1740, with three months
of snow and ice. In 1981, one local remembers 'a
pretty bad winter in Milton Keynes... Although the
schools remained open, they were damn cold – there
was no heating on. We sat in class with coats and
scarves on.' One skier was undaunted, however,
exploiting the slopes of the V8 Marlborough Street
grid-road in CMK.

(Photograph courtesy of Living Archive)

THE SNOW DOME. A winter view from Campbell Park with the Peace Pagoda (right); what locals call the Snow Dome is top centre. The nation's first 'SNO!zone' opened in 2001 in CMK as part of a centre incorporating a sixteen-screen cinema, a bowling alley, two climbing walls, thirteen bars and restaurants and a night-club for 2,000. The centre receives over a million visitors a year. When the indoor snow slopes opened, they were the longest in Europe – 170m, with a 135m training slope – all covered by 1½ tonnes of real snow maintained at -2°C. In 2009, members of the British Antarctic Survey Team tested a new pyramid tent at SNO!zone for use in the Antarctic. *(Photograph courtesy of The Parks Trust)*

MILTON KEYNES MARKETS

LIVESTOCK MARKET, BLETCHLEY, *c.*1912. Even in 1963 the Bletchley Market sold 100 cattle, 800 sheep and 150 pigs a week. Prospective buyers would 'give their secret nod or blink of the eye when placing a bid', remembers one local. For new settlers from post-war London, the market was 'the highlight of the week... The children loved to see the calves, though it looked a bit cruel, clipping their ears.' Another recalls: 'They'd auction live chickens... It had to be killed before you left – you'd pay the auctioneer's assistant 3*d* to wring its neck, so you had to pluck it and gut it yourself.' *(Photograph courtesy of Living Archive)*

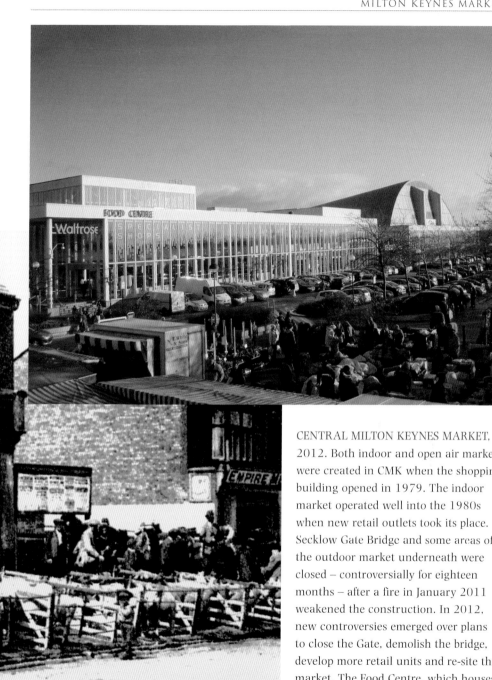

CENTRAL MILTON KEYNES MARKET, 2012. Both indoor and open air markets were created in CMK when the shopping building opened in 1979. The indoor market operated well into the 1980s when new retail outlets took its place. Secklow Gate Bridge and some areas of the outdoor market underneath were closed – controversially for eighteen months – after a fire in January 2011 weakened the construction. In 2012, new controversies emerged over plans to close the Gate, demolish the bridge, develop more retail units and re-site the market. The Food Centre, which houses a supermarket, a freezer centre and a range of specialist shops, was opened by Princess Anne in 1988.
(Photograph courtesy of Bob Hill)

QUEEN'S COURT

QUEEN'S COURT, 1979. Lord Campbell, MKDC chairman, accompanies the Queen and Fred Roche, MKDC general manager, is to the right of Prince Phillip. Originally, Garden Court (renamed to commemorate the Queen's visit) had a pool where water flowed evenly over its Cornish granite edges – a masterly piece of precision engineering. It was also meticulously designed with a unique geometry relating not only to the dimensions of the city's grid and the shopping building of which it was an integral part, but also to the city centre's alignment with midsummer and midwinter sunrises and sunsets. Both the pool and the original pergolas were set out on that geometry, enhanced by an 8ft-diameter sundial to tell the time of day and year.
(*Photograph courtesy of Living Archive*)

QUEEN'S COURT, 2011. A recent £10 million development has created new restaurants, winter garden colonnades and a courtyard providing opportunities such as enjoyed by these skaters. The shopping building itself – now thecentre:mk – attracted 250,000 people a week by its first Christmas, from as far as Carlisle. Now, around 30 million visitors a year (600,000 shoppers weekly) come to shop. A listed building, it is ranked in the ten best UK shopping centres for attractiveness – with its naturally lit and clean, wide marbled arcades; its tropical plants and airy atmosphere; and its 'astonishing purity of form' (Robert Maxwell, architect). With Midsummer Place at its west end, visitors have around 300 shops to explore, and 50 places to eat and drink.
(Photograph courtesy of Bob Hill)

CHRIST THE CORNERSTONE CHURCH, CENTRAL MILTON KEYNES

CITY CHURCH DOME, 1990. Milton Keynes built the first city-centre ecumenical church in Britain – the Church of Christ the Cornerstone. Dedicated at a special service in 1992 attended by the Queen, the ceremony was performed by the four presidents of 'Churches Together in England' – the Archbishop of Canterbury, the Most Reverend and Right Honourable George Carey of the Church of England; the Reverend Desmond Pemberton of the Wesleyan Holiness Church; the Reverend Dr John Newton of the Methodist Church; and His Eminence Cardinal Basil Hume, Archbishop of Westminster – whose sermon at the ceremony was the first by a Roman Catholic Cardinal before a reigning monarch for 400 years.
(Photograph courtesy of MKDC/CNT/EP archive)

CHRIST THE CORNERSTONE, 2012. Celebrating its twentieth anniversary in 2012, the church's main function continues: five different denominations – the Baptist Union, the Church of England, Methodist, Roman Catholic and United Reform Churches 'are covenanted together' to share worship, understanding, and service to others. It is also the venue for concerts, conferences, dances, weddings, toddlers' groups, training courses, blood donor sessions, an Asian lunch club, Weightwatchers and appeals tribunals. With over 130,000 visitors a year, the church's volunteers are an invaluable support – on reception, in the shop, as a guide for tours, or in the café.
(Photograph courtesy of Bob Hill)

FROM 'AM-DRAM' TO PROFESSIONAL THEATRE

AMATEUR DRAMATICS, *c.*1950. Milton Keynes' designated area hosted many amateur dramatic groups through the years – like this one at the Science Arts Institute Wolverton. They ranged from the 'Penny Gaff' – a travelling company of players visiting New Bradwell in

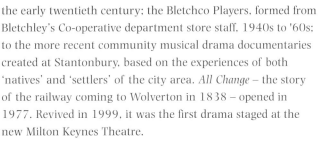

the early twentieth century; the Bletchco Players, formed from
Bletchley's Co-operative department store staff, 1940s to '60s;
to the more recent community musical drama documentaries
created at Stantonbury, based on the experiences of both
'natives' and 'settlers' of the city area. *All Change* – the story
of the railway coming to Wolverton in 1838 – opened in
1977. Revived in 1999, it was the first drama staged at the
new Milton Keynes Theatre.
(Photograph courtesy of Living Archive)

MILTON KEYNES THEATRE, 2006. Now, in addition to
twenty-two local amateur theatre groups, Milton Keynes hosts
the most successful provincial theatre in the country with around
80 per cent audience occupancy. Its state-of-the-art equipment
allows deaf people to hear and its auditorium ceiling to move up
or down to suit capacities of up to 1,300 people. Opera, drama,
musicals, dance, concerts and comedy are presented in an
auditorium that is the envy of other cities 'and on a stage that
is loved by the companies who perform there' (Roy Nevitt). The
resident Milton Keynes City Orchestra complements a programme
that includes West End shows, the Royal Shakespeare Company
and the Glyndebourne Touring Opera.
(Photograph courtesy of Shaun Webb Design, www.swd-uk.com)

FROM
OLD-TIME
DANCING TO
HEN PARTIES

CRAUFORD ARMS, WOLVERTON, *c.*1950. These
old-time dancers were a contrast to the new fashion of
entertainment then just emerging. A local band – Terry
Carroll and the Rockets – also played at the Crauford
Arms. One resident remembers: 'They played a lot of
rock 'n' roll stuff – Bill Haley and early Elvis Presley.
Girls sat down the sides and blokes by the bar. The girls
would wait for a dance... I couldn't do anything until
I'd had two or three pints.' Another recalls: 'The best
dances were the Boxing Day dances at the Crauford
– very well attended. There was generally a fight, but a
lot of the time it was just fists.'
(Photograph courtesy of Living Archive)

HEN PARTY, CMK, 2009. On Friday, 3 July 2009, Living Archive – Milton Keynes' creative cultural and community development agency – conducted a 'Mass Observation'. They asked people in Central Milton Keynes to record their day. Some wrote diaries, some took photographs, some filled in questionnaires. People were interviewed and filmed to archive their 'tale' of living or working in Milton Keynes. A subsequent exhibition by 'Discover Milton Keynes' and on Facebook shows the results of that day and captures a 'day in the life' of the city. This Hen Party was one of those featured. Other activities on offer for such groups included ice-skating, skydiving, go-karting and paint-balling.

(Photograph courtesy of Living Archive)

FROM PENNY FARTHINGS
TO REDWAY CYCLING

MAZEPRO CYCLING CLUB, *c.* 1890. The Penny Farthing – so called because of its different-sized wheels – was constructed in metal in around the 1880s. With pedals directly attached to the large front wheel and solid rubber tyres, it provided a thrillingly fast ride. But the rider could not slow the bike and was likely to be launched over the handlebars onto his head if a rut was encountered, or something stuck in the spokes – hence the expression 'breakneck speed'. By 1900, subsequent

bicycles – the 'hobbyhorse' and 'bone-shaker' – became easier to ride with lower pedals, chains and pneumatic tyres. The Cycling Tourist Club, founded in 1878 to promote bicycle travel and defend cyclists' rights, spawned local clubs, such as shown here in Wolverton.
(*Photograph courtesy of Living Archive*)

CYCLING THE REDWAYS, 2005. Milton Keynes' cycling clubs can enjoy four customised Heritage Trails. These pass the city's lakes, its ancient villages and its new public art works. Milton Keynes also hosts two National Cycle Network routes and national events from the Milk Race, 1978, to the Tour of Britain, 2009. Its unique local Redways network – identified by red tarmac surfaces – currently totals over 270km (200 miles) in length, of which 70km (45 miles) are leisure routes. Their function – to keep cycles off the grid-roads – creates some debate amongst cycling enthusiasts, but as one former MK resident says: 'It's a million miles better than cycling in Manchester!'
(*Photograph courtesy of The Parks Trust*)

FROM STREET ART TO PUBLIC ART COLLECTION

BILL BILLINGS' WORKSHOP, 1981. Bill Billings (1938-2007) was a lorry driver who came to work on the new city's building sites. He was also a poet, playwright, painter, musician and community artist. He created one of Milton Keynes' most famous and earliest public art icons, the Dinosaur at Peartree Bridge. He was a master at creating concrete sculptures that were both wonderful to look at and robust enough to withstand the roughest treatment. Formerly from the SAS, Bill introduced street-art to thousands of people from all walks of life, including prisoners – and, as here, for handicapped people. His services to the community earned him an Honorary Degree from the OU in 1986 and an MBE in 2000. *(Photograph courtesy of Living Archive)*

CHAIN REACTION, 2005. This Ray Smith sculpture was installed in 1992 in Campbell Park alongside Silbury Boulevard. Before the new city was built, there were few artworks accessible to people in the area – as in most places outside big conurbations. However, Milton Keynes has become home to the UK's largest collection of contemporary urban sculpture with over 200 works of art in public places. Famous examples include Black Horse by Dame Elisabeth Frink; Octo, Essence and Equatorial Sundial, by Wendy Taylor CBE; and The Whisper by Andre Wallace. Milton Keynes Gallery opened in 1999 with an exhibition by Gilbert and George. Now, its three galleries hold around ten exhibitions every year, free to the public.
(Photograph courtesy of The Parks Trust).

THE PEOPLE OF
MILTON KEYNES

DINNER TIME AT Wolverton Works, *c.* 1910. In the thirty years to 1871, the population around the Works rose eight-fold. By 1901, it was 9,200 – larger than Aylesbury or Buckingham. The largest employer, the railway dominated both demography and culture, as one local recalls: 'My father, born in 1901, became a coach painter at the Works and received a chiming mantle clock to mark fifty years' service. He'd walk the mile to work every day, returning home at midday for his dinner. The road was filled with hundreds of men in cloth caps with the Works hooter calling

them to work. He bred canaries which he kept in aviary at the bottom of the garden and also had an allotment...'
(Photograph courtesy of Living Archive)

RACE FOR LIFE, 2005. Around 25 per cent of MK's population is under eighteen years; half is under thirty-five – three years younger than the nation's average. In 2011, in a population of 255,780, many were families with young children. With more than 5,200 workplaces and 151,000 jobs, unemployment stood at less than 2 per cent and 29 per cent of the workforce was in skilled, managerial and professional categories. Milton Keynes' young and dynamic demographic has perhaps given the city its energy and vibrancy. As settler Roger Kitchen says: 'Lots of people have been able to shape their own destiny here... It's open, it's pioneering. That's why we're fiercely patriotic about the place. And we can, we can make a difference.'
(Photograph courtesy of The Parks Trust)

If you enjoyed this book, you may also be interested in…

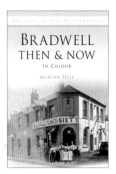

Bradwell Then & Now
MARION HILL

Over the centuries, Bradwell has definitely seen its fair share of change, but its past and present remain inextricably linked. In this vivid full-colour book, Marion Hill's collection of archive and modern photographs alongside her many fascinating stories chart the history of the town, from Roman settlers to a disused railway line now threading a modern route as a cycle path. *Bradwell Then & Now* will surely prove irresistible for anyone who values the unique heritage of this historic place.

978 0 7524 6319 3

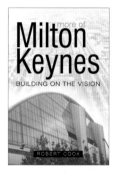

More of Milton Keynes: Building on the Vision
ROBERT COOK

Milton Keynes has been designated one of the four potential growth areas in the south-east of England. There are plans to build up to 70,000 new homes in the city before 2031, and also develop transport infrastructure. Here, Robert Cook examines the history of Milton Keynes so far, and also explores surrounding towns and villages.

978 0 7509 3859 4

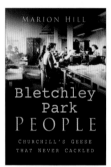

Bletchley Park People
MARION HILL

The British government's top secret Code & Cypher School at Bletchley Park, otherwise known as Station X, was the unlikely setting for one of the most vital undercover operations of the Second World War. It was at Bletchley in present-day Milton Keynes that teams of code breakers succeeded in cracking Germany's supposedly unbreakable Enigma codes, thereby shortening the war by at least two years. A selection of archive photographs and illustrations accompany this fascinating text.

978 0 7509 3362 9

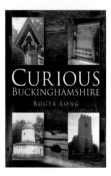

Curious Buckinghamshire
ROGER LONG

A guide to over 100 unusual and extraordinary sights from all parts of the county. Featured here are tales of unsolved murders, witchcraft, hangings, poltergeists, 'cunning men', underground caves, backswording and riots, as well as myths, legends and folklore from around Buckinghamshire. Illustrated with a range of photographs and original drawings. Roger Long's entertaining stories will inspire Buckinghamshire residents and visitors alike.

978 0 7524 5516 7

Visit our website and discover thousands of other History Press books.
www.thehistorypress.co.uk